Sally

Lehrwerk für den Englischunterricht ab Klasse 1

Pupil's Book 4

Erarbeitet von
Martina Bredenbröcker
Jasmin Brune
Daniela Elsner
Barbara Gleich
Stefanie Gleixner-Weyrauch
Simone Gutwerk
Marion Lugauer
Sabine Schwarz

Unter Beratung von Jane Brockmann-Fairchild

Illustriert von
Monica May, Wilfried Poll,
Anja Boretzki, Andreas Fischer,
Thilo Pustlauk und Gisela Vogel

Oldenbourg

Inhalt

Special days:

pupil's CD / teacher's CD

teacher's CD only

Write.

Draw.

Speak.

Rap: Welcome back to school!

Susan

Step to the left, step to the right.
Raise your  and feel alright.
Turn around and say: "That's cool!"
Welcome back to school!

Tim

Eric

Sit on your , write in the air.
Let's have fun with English.
Dance to the beat and say: "That's cool!"
Welcome back to school!

Emily

Around the classroom you must look.
Put your  on the .
Turn around and say: "That's cool!"
Welcome back to school!

Liz

Phil

Listen and sing.

Let's play a board game!

Play in groups (2–5).
Roll the dice. Take turns.

Red number:
Do what it says or answer the question.
If you can't, miss a turn.

The winner is the first to reach finish.

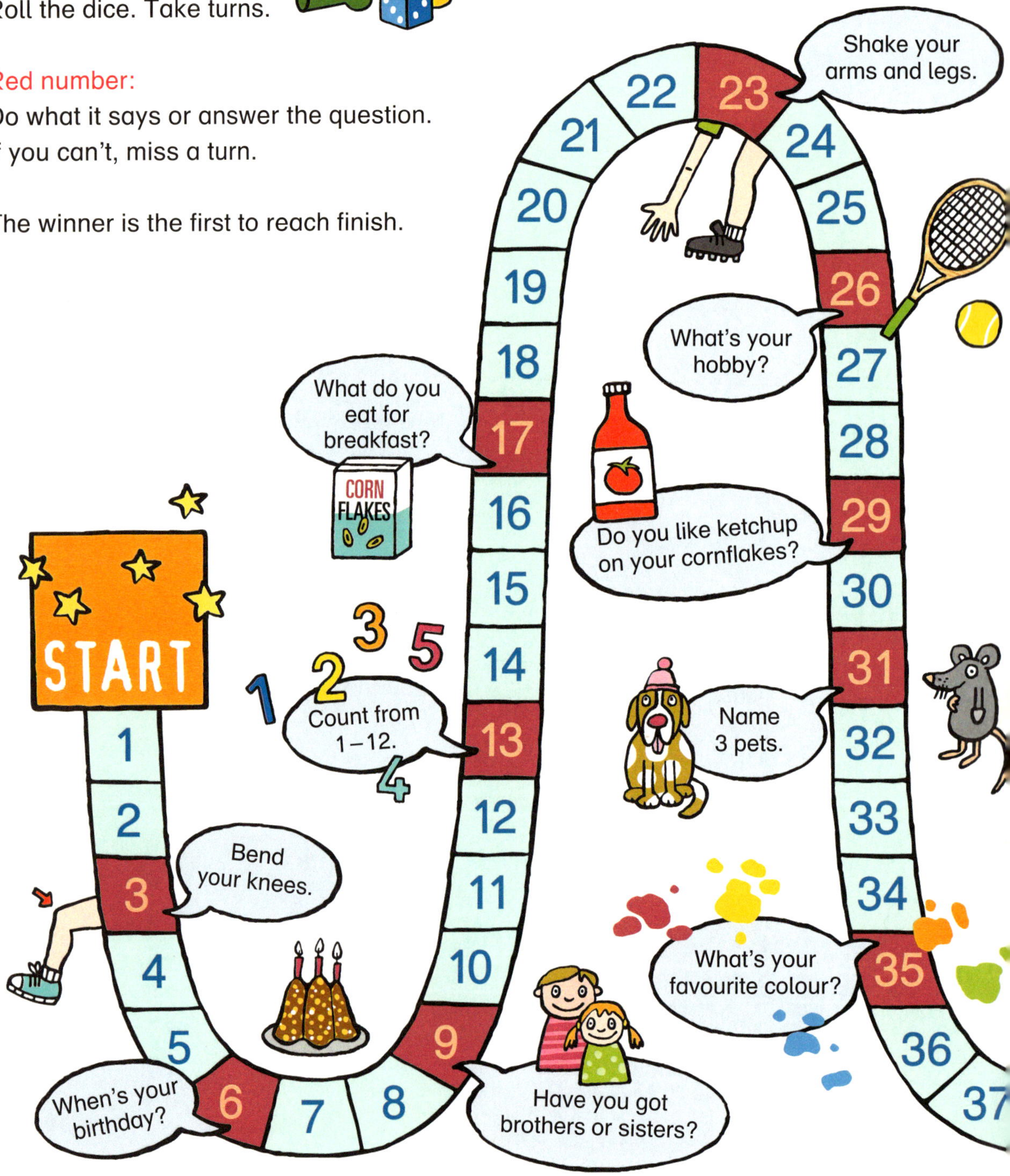

If you don't know a word, look it up in your word list.
FINISH
MAY 5 MON
Name the days of the week.
52
53
54
51
50
55
Stand on one leg for 30 seconds.
49
56
48
57
What's your favourite toy?
Say a rhyme or sing a song.
47
58
80
79
78
What's your telephone number?
46
59
77
45
Name 5 things in your classroom.
60
76
44
Sing a birthday song.
75
61
Name 5 different kinds of fruit.
43
62
74
42
63
How do you feel today?
73
41
What's the weather like today?
64
72
40
65
71
Who is this?
39
Show me your socks. What colour are they?
66
70
38
What's the name of your best friend?
67
68
69

Our home is too small

1. Listen to the story and point.
2. Look at the house and speak.
   The living room is too small …
3. Draw your dream house.
   Write about it.

My dream house
has got a big garden,
seven bedrooms ...

Tim and Susan's new house

1. Listen, find Susan's furniture and point.
2. What furniture has Susan got?
   Susan has got brown shelves, a purple sofa …
3. What furniture have you got in your room?
   I've got …

Let's make Sally's sandwich!

Take a slice of bread.
Put it on a plate.

Spread ketchup and mustard on it.

Cut the tomato and the cucumber.
Put them on the bread.

Put some ham, cheese and lettuce on it.

Put another slice of bread on top.

Cut the sandwich in half. Sally's sandwich is ready to eat!

What do you want to put on your sandwich?
Make a list.

In the dining hall

It's Monday.

It's Tuesday.

It's Thursday.

It's Friday.

1. Listen and read.
2. Write about Phil's menu plan.
   On Monday Phil has salad with cheese and a glass of water.
   On Tuesday he has ...

Emily's day

At 8 o'clock I get up and have breakfast.

School begins at 9 o'clock.

At 12 o'clock I have lunch.

At 3 o'clock I go home.

At 4 o'clock I do my homework.

At 5 o'clock I call my friends and we play football.

At 6 o'clock I have dinner.

At 8 o'clock I read a book or watch TV.

At 9 o'clock I go to bed. Good night!

1. Listen, look and read.
2. What about your day? Tell your partner what you do.
   In the morning …
   In the afternoon …
   In the evening / At night …
3. And what do you do on a Sunday?

MY SUNDAY
On Sunday I get up …

Hobbies

riding a horse | riding a mountain bike | playing the guitar
reading books | ice skating | playing the piano | snowboarding
playing football | swimming

skipping

1. What are their hobbies? Look and speak.
   Tim's hobby is …
2. What's your hobby?
   My hobby is …
3. Hobbies in your class:
   Make a list and do a class survey.

The interview

1. Ask your partner.

Can you	play football	
	sing a song	
	play the guitar	?
	ride a skateboard	
	do inline skating	

2. Listen to the interview with Dirk Nowitzki.

Dirk Nowitzki is playing basketball.

3. Do your own interview.

4. Say the tongue twister.

In the supermarket

1. Listen and point.

2. Make your own shopping list.
   I want to buy two bottles of orange juice,
   a box of biscuits ...

At the shopping centre

1. Where can you buy these things?

In the
- book shop
- sports shop
- music shop
- supermarket
- toy shop
- sweet shop
- shoe shop

I can buy

2. Design your own shopping centre.

Jack and the beanstalk

1. Listen, look and point.
2. Act out the story together.

Let's act it out!

Reading and learning the story

Painting the background

Making the music

Telling the story with shadow puppets

Practising the story

Performing the story

The Wright Brothers

The Wright Brothers made bikes.

The Wright Brothers made kites.

The Wright Brothers made planes.

The Wright Brothers became famous with the "Wright Model B".

1. Look and read.

a bike saucer

a one-wheeled car

a flying sledge

2. Look at Gyro Gearloose's fantasy vehicles.
   Draw your own fantasy vehicle.

In the plane

No smoking!

Fasten your seat belts, please!

Switch off your mobile phones, radios and laptops!

Put your seats in an upright position!

1. Listen and point.
2. Draw your own sign. Ask your partner: What is it?

Transport in London

left-hand traffic with double-decker buses

a taxi

an entrance to the underground trains

a ferry on the River Thames

3. Look at the photos. What's different in England?

Detective Brighthead

1. Listen to the story and look at the pictures.

2. What forms of transport does Mr Brighthead take? He takes the ...

Detective Brighthead's trip to the jungle

1. Where are the animals?
   Ask your partner.

   Is the zebra next to the snake?
   Is the hippo behind the elephant? …

in on next to in front of
behind under

Yes, it is.

No, it isn't. It's …

2. Make a poster.

The clever tortoise

Listen, look and read.

The five minute zoo game

Play with a partner.

Roll the dice.

Play for five minutes.

Take turns.

The winner is the player who has got the most points.

Move in any direction.

Animal picture:
Name the animal = 1 point.
Name the animal and describe it = 2 points.

Snack stop: You must pay.
Miss a turn.

Crocodile: Bad luck!
You lose 1 point.

At the doctor's

1. Read.

2. Why do the animals run away each time? Look at the green door.

The inline skating accident

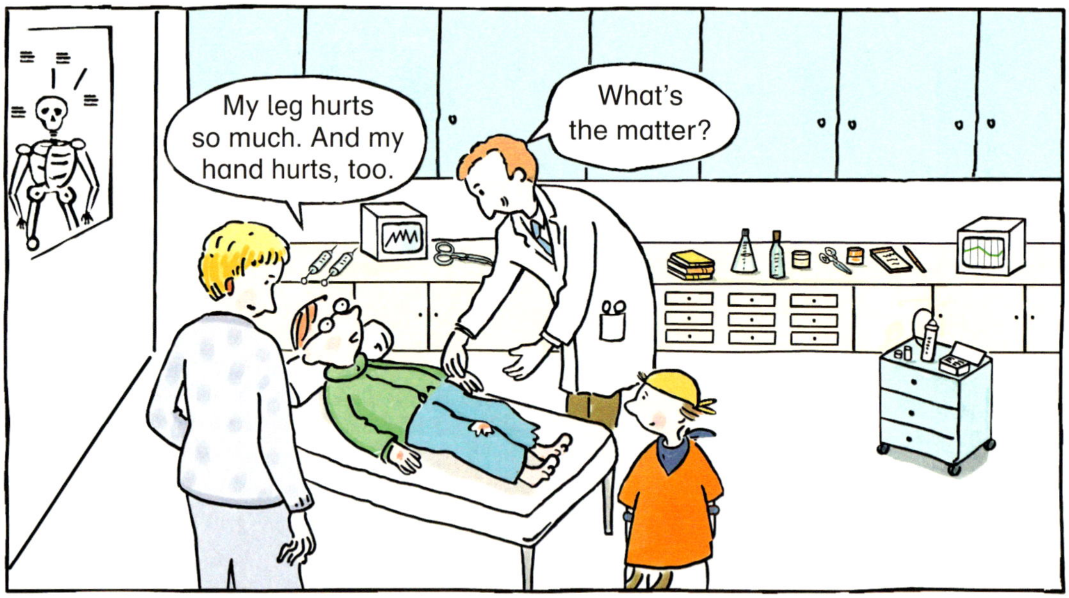

1. Look and speak.
2. Look at the waiting room.
   What's the matter?
   Write a sentence about each patient.
   The boy has got a headache ...

headache
neckache
earache
backache

Sally and the Loch Ness Monster

Listen, look and read.

A holiday trip to Scotland

1. Look and speak. Mr Brown wants to see …
2. Make a poster or a collage about Scotland. Find out and learn about Scotland on the internet.
3. Where do you want to go for your holidays?

Scottish dance

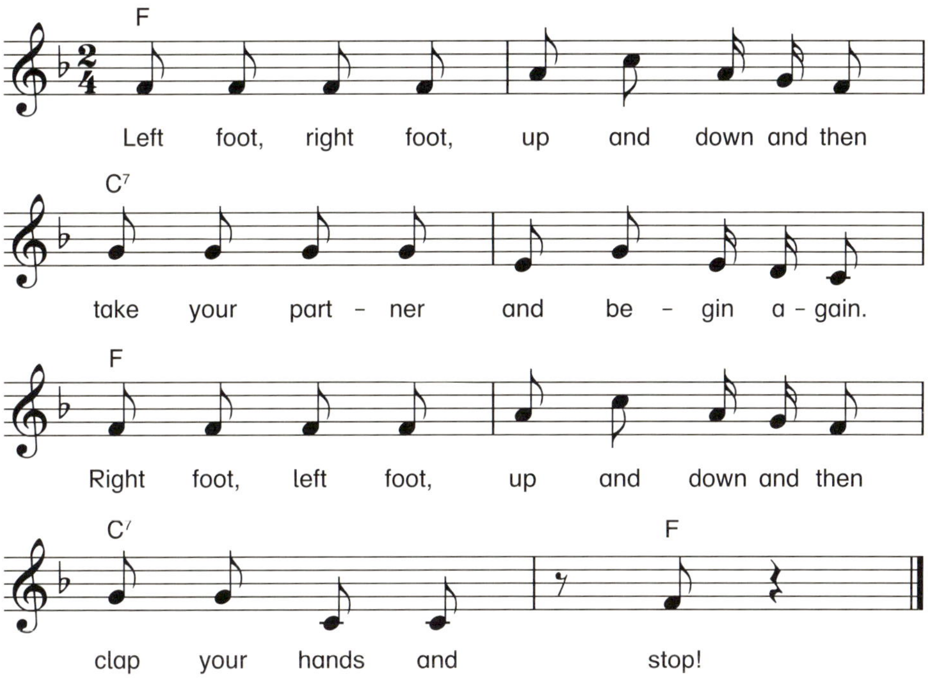

Listen, sing and dance.

What do you want to be?

shop assistant

hairdresser

teacher

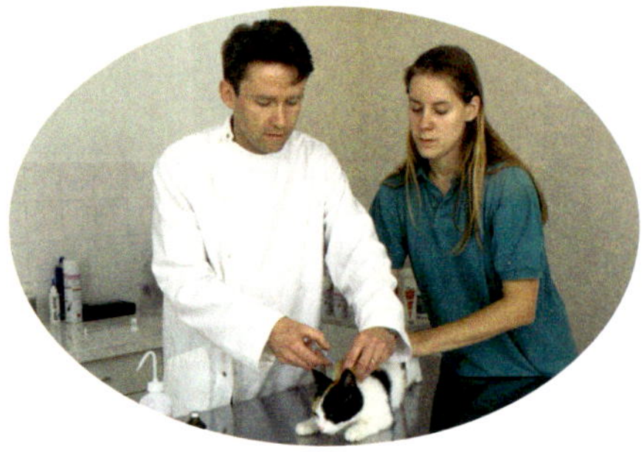

vet

policewoman

football player

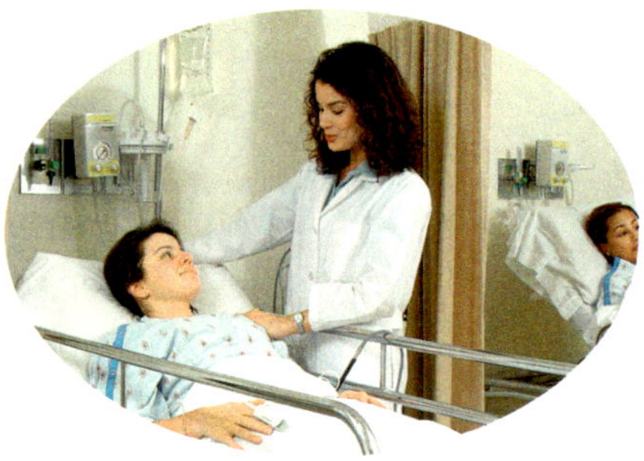

doctor

1. Listen and point.

2. What do you want to be?
   I want to be a …

3. Do a job survey in your class.
   Make a chart.

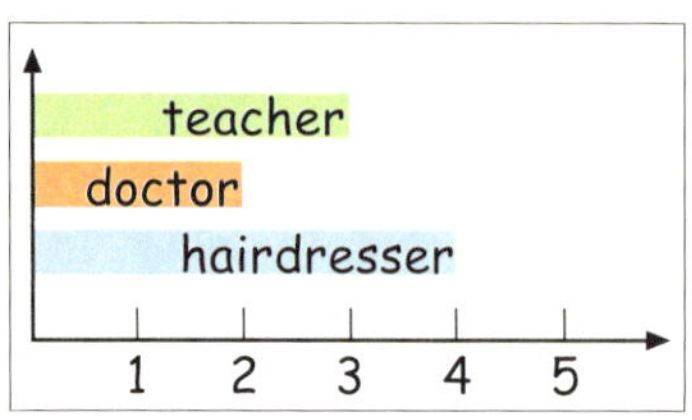

My jobs

And what are your jobs?
I have to …

My cat likes to hide in boxes

France

Japan

Spain

Berlin, Germany

Greece

1. Listen and look.
2. Mime one of the cats.
   Let your partner guess.

We all live in the same world

Hola!

Juanita

Bonjour!

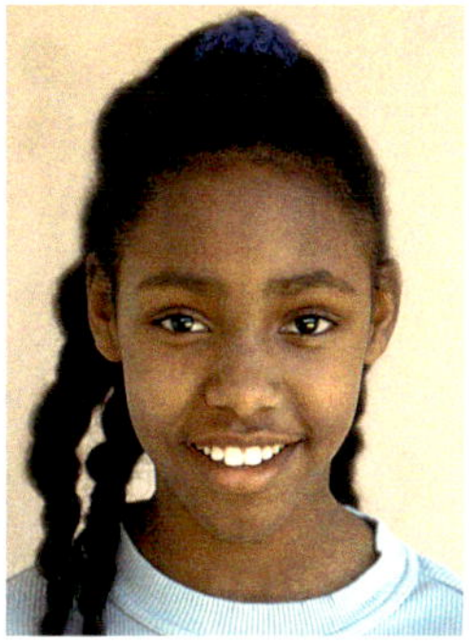

Jacqueline

Ciao!

Paolo

Hello!

Thomas

Hallo!

Maria

Merhaba!

Güler

Jassu!

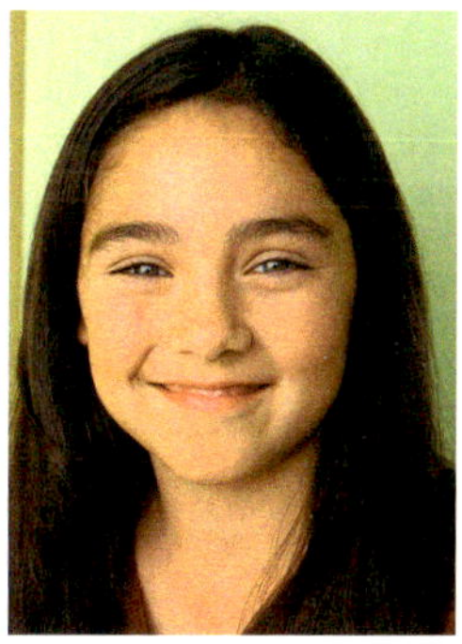

Dimitra

Priwjet!

Sergej

But we all laugh in the same language.
We all like to sing and play.
We all live in the same world,
no matter where we're from.

1. Listen and sing.
2. What's the word for Hello! in different languages?
   Make a list.

Looking for a penfriend

Datei Bearbeiten Ansicht Favoriten Extras ?

Zurück Suchen Favoriten

Adresse Wechseln zu Links

Find a penfriend!

I'm a boy / girl. I'm 8 / 9 / 10 years old. I'm from Germany / England / Australia.

My hobby is snowboarding.

I'm looking for a boy / girl. Age: 8 / 9 / 10 Country: USA / Germany / Spain

Carlos: boy, 10 years old, Spain

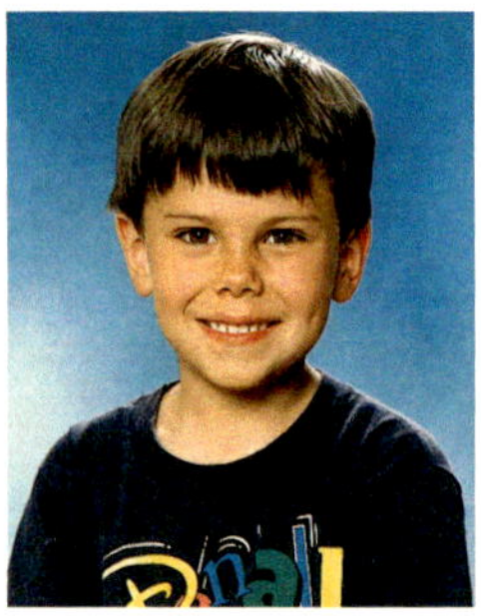

Hi, I'm Carlos. I'm from Spain.
I'm 10 years old.
My hobbies are skateboarding, reading comics and swimming.
I can speak Spanish, German and English.
I'm looking for a penfriend from England.

Internet

1. Listen. What is Phil looking for? Tell your class.
   He's looking for a … from …

2. Are you looking for a penfriend, too? Tell your partner.

   Yes, I'm looking for a …

   No, I don't want a penfriend.

3. Write a letter to Carlos.

   Dear Carlos,
   I'm …

Guy Fawkes Day – Bonfire Night

Light the fire, light the fire.
Let it burn, let it burn.
Bonfire, bonfire.
Guy Fawkes Day, Guy Fawkes Day.

Sizzle, whistle, sizzle, whistle.
Crackle, rumble, crackle, rumble.
Boom, bang, boom, bang.
Fireworks, fireworks.

1. Listen and sing.
2. Write the seasons in the correct order.
   spring, ...

winter summer
autumn spring

Thanksgiving today

Mum gets up at 6 o'clock
in the morning.
She puts the turkey into the oven.
The turkey takes five hours to cook.

At 12 o'clock my grandpa,
my grandma, my aunt and
my cousins come to our house.
We have our Thanksgiving dinner.

In the afternoon we go to the
Thanksgiving parade.

In the evening we watch the football
match on TV.

Listen, look and read.

A story about the first Thanksgiving

1. What do you know about the American Indians?
2. What is Sally writing?

Come to the USA!

New York and the Statue of Liberty

Disney World, Florida (fun park)

a cowboy at work

Bryce Canyon National Park, Utah

a cable car in San Francisco

Venice Beach, Los Angeles

1. Look at the photos.
2. Make a poster or a collage about the USA.
   Find out and learn about the USA on the internet.

Father Christmas in Australia

1. Listen and point.
2. Read.

The five days of Christmas

kookaburra

On the first day of Christmas
my true love sent to me
a  in a gum tree.

On the second day of Christmas
my true love sent to me
two small 
and a  in a gum tree.

koala

cockatoo

On the third day of Christmas
my true love sent to me
three ,
two small …

On the fourth day of Christmas
my true love sent to me
four ,
three …

crocodile

kangaroo

On the fifth day of Christmas
my true love sent to me
five ,
four …

1. Look at the photos. Listen and sing.

2. Write word cards for a Christmas bingo.
sleigh, reindeer, stocking, present, star,
Christmas tree, winter, cold, snowy…

Christmas in Australia

Let's go to Australia!

Sydney is the biggest city.

A road train is a very long truck.

Ayers Rock is a big flat rock.

At the Great Barrier Reef
you can see under water corals
and wonderful coloured fish.

An Australian Aborigine
is playing the didgeridoo.

1. Look at the photos.
2. Listen and point.
3. Read the text. Find the correct photo.
4. Draw an Australian traffic sign.

Let's make an Easter bunny mosaic card!

You need:
coloured eggshells
cardboard
a pencil
glue
scissors

Break the eggshells into small pieces.

Draw your Easter bunny on the cardboard. Cut it out.

Glue the eggshells down to make your mosaic bunny.

Glue your Easter bunny onto the cardboard. Write an Easter greeting on your card.

Write word cards for an Easter bingo.
bunny, egg, tree, flower, grass,
spring, warm, cloudy, sunny, ...

Words

Africa Afrika
afternoon der Nachmittag
America Amerika
I am ich bin
angry wütend
animal das Tier
animal centre das Tierheim
apple der Apfel
April der April
they are sie sind
we are wir sind
you are du bist, ihr seid
arm der Arm
arrow der Pfeil
Asia Asien
August der August
aunt die Tante
Australia Australien
autumn der Herbst
away weg

backache die Rückenschmerzen
bacon der Speck
bad schlecht, schlimm
ball der Ball
banana die Banane
basket der Korb
bat die Fledermaus
bathroom das Badezimmer
to be sein
beach der Strand
beach ball der Wasserball
bean die Bohne
beanstalk die Bohnenranke
bear der Bär
bed das Bett
bedroom das Schlafzimmer
behind hinter
to bend beugen
big groß
bird der Vogel
birthday der Geburtstag
biscuit der Keks
black schwarz
blood das Blut
blue blau
board die Tafel
body der Körper
book das Buch
boot der Stiefel
bottle die Flasche
bow der Bogen
box (boxes) die Schachtel (die Schachteln), die Kiste (die Kisten)
boy der Junge
bread das Brot
breakfast das Frühstück
brother der Bruder
brown braun
to brush bürsten
budgie der Wellensittich
bus (buses) der Bus (die Busse)
butter die Butter
to buy kaufen

cake der Kuchen
to call rufen, anrufen
can können
can't nicht können
Canada Kanada
candle die Kerze
cap die Kappe

Words

car das Auto
card die Karte
carrot die Karotte, die Möhre
castle das Schloss, die Burg
cat die Katze
to catch fangen
chair der Stuhl
chalk die Kreide
cheap billig
cheese der Käse
cherry (cherries) die Kirsche (die Kirschen)
child das Kind
children die Kinder
chimney der Schornstein
chocolate bar der Schokoriegel
Christmas Weihnachten
Christmas tree der Weihnachtsbaum, der Christbaum
to clap klatschen
class die Klasse
to clean putzen
clever schlau, klug
to climb klettern, hochklettern
(one) o'clock (ein) Uhr
clothes die Kleidung
cloud die Wolke
cloudy bewölkt
coat der Mantel
coffee der Kaffee
coke die Cola
cold kalt
colour die Farbe
to colour anmalen
to come kommen
computer der Computer
computer game das Computerspiel
cookie der Keks
corn der Mais
cornflakes die Cornflakes
costume die Verkleidung
to count zählen
cousin der Cousin, die Cousine
cow die Kuh
cucumber die Gurke
a cup of ... eine Tasse ...
cupboard der Schrank
to cut schneiden

to dance tanzen
dark dunkel
day der Tag
December der Dezember
desk der Schreibtisch
dice der Würfel
dirty schmutzig
to do machen, tun
to do magic zaubern
doctor der Arzt
dog der Hund
doll die Puppe
door die Tür
down hinunter
to draw zeichnen
dress das Kleid
drink das Getränk
to drink trinken
duck die Ente

ear das Ohr
earache die Ohrenschmerzen
Easter Ostern
Easter bunny der Osterhase
Easter egg das Osterei
to eat essen
egg das Ei
eight acht

Words

elephant der Elefant
eleven elf
England England
English englisch
Englishman der Engländer
Europe Europa
evening der Abend
exercise die Übung
expensive teuer
eye das Auge

fairy die Fee
family die Familie
farm animal das Bauernhoftier
fast schnell
fat dick, fett
father der Vater
Father Christmas der Weihnachtsmann
favourite (pet) Lieblings(tier)
February der Februar
to feed füttern
feet die Füße
ferry die Fähre
to fill füllen
fine gut, schön
finger der Finger
fireplace der Kamin
fish der Fisch, die Fische
five fünf
floor der Fußboden
flower die Blume
fly die Fliege
to fly fliegen
fog der Nebel
foggy nebelig
folder der Schnellhefter
food das Essen
foot der Fuß
football der Fußball
forest der Wald
fork die Gabel
four vier
France Frankreich
Friday der Freitag
friend der Freund, die Freundin
friendly freundlich
frog der Frosch
fruit die Frucht, das Obst
fruit salad der Obstsalat
fun der Spaß
funny lustig, komisch

game das Spiel
garage die Garage
garden der Garten
German deutsch
Germany Deutschland
to get up aufstehen
ghost der Geist
giraffe die Giraffe
girl das Mädchen
a glass of ... ein Glas ...
glue der Kleber
to go gehen, fahren
good gut
goose die Gans
grandfather der Großvater
grandmother die Großmutter
grass das Gras
Great Britain Großbritannien
green grün
grey grau
guard die Wache
guinea pig das Meerschweinchen
guitar die Gitarre

Words

hair das Haar
Halloween Halloween
ham der Schinken
hamster der Hamster
hand die Hand
happy glücklich
hat der Hut
to have (got) haben
to have (lunch) (zu Mittag) essen
head der Kopf
headache die Kopfschmerzen
to help helfen
hen die Henne
hill der Hügel
hippo das Nilpferd
holidays die Ferien
hobby (hobbies) das Hobby (die Hobbys)
home das Heim, das Zuhause
at home zu Hause
homework die Hausaufgaben
honey der Honig
horse das Pferd
hot chocolate der Kakao
hot heiß
house das Haus
hungry hungrig
to hurt wehtun

ice cream das Eis
ice skating das Schlittschuhfahren
in front of vor
in in
inline skates die Inlineskates
insect das Insekt

jacket die Jacke
jam die Marmelade
January der Januar
Japan Japan
jeans die Jeans
job die Arbeit, die Aufgabe
July der Juli
to jump springen
June der Juni

kangaroo das Känguru
ketchup das Ketchup
king der König
kitchen die Küche
knee das Knie
knife (knives) das Messer (die Messer)
to knock klopfen
to know wissen, kennen

Words

ladder die Leiter
lake der See
lamp die Lampe
leaf (leaves) das Blatt (die Blätter)
to learn lernen
left links
leg das Bein
lemon die Zitrone
lemonade die Limonade
letter der Brief
lettuce der Kopfsalat
to like mögen
lion der Löwe
to listen (to) zuhören
little klein
to live leben, wohnen
living room das Wohnzimmer
to love lieben, sehr mögen
lunch das Mittagessen

magic (beans) Zauber(bohnen)
to make machen
March der März
market der Markt
May der Mai
meadow die Wiese
to meet treffen, begegnen
melon die Melone
mice die Mäuse
milk die Milch
mitten der Fäustling
Monday der Montag
money das Geld
monkey der Affe
month der Monat
monster das Ungeheuer
moon der Mond
morning der Morgen
mother die Mutter
mountain der Berg
mountain bike das Mountainbike
mouse die Maus
mouth der Mund
to move (sich) bewegen
must müssen
mustard der Senf

name der Name
neckache die Nackenschmerzen
new neu
New Zealand Neuseeland
next to neben
night die Nacht
nine neun
nose die Nase
November der November
number die Zahl

October der Oktober
old alt
on auf
one eins
orange die Orange; orange
orange juice der Orangensaft

Words

to paint malen
palace der Palast
parents die Eltern
park der Park
to pay bezahlen
pear die Birne
pen der Füller
pencil der Bleistift
pencil case das Mäppchen
people die Leute, die Menschen
pepper der Pfeffer
pet das Haustier
piano das Klavier
picture das Bild
pie die Pastete, der Kuchen
pig das Schwein
pineapple die Ananas
pink rosa
plane das Flugzeug
plate der Teller
to play spielen
player der Spieler
please bitte
plum die Pflaume
pond der Teich
poor arm
potato (potatoes)
die Kartoffel (die Kartoffeln)
present das Geschenk
prince der Prinz
princess die Prinzessin
pullover der Pullover
pumpkin der Kürbis
pupil der Schüler
purple lila
to put setzen, stellen, legen
to put on anziehen

queen die Königin

rabbit das Kaninchen
rain der Regen
rainy regnerisch
to read lesen
red rot
reindeer das Rentier, die Rentiere
rich reich
to ride fahren, reiten
right rechts
river der Fluss
roll das Brötchen, die Semmel
room das Zimmer
rubber der Radiergummi
ruler das Lineal
to run rennen, laufen

sad traurig
salt das Salz
sand der Sand
sandwich das Sandwich
Saturday der Samstag
scared erschrocken, ängstlich
scarf der Schal
school die Schule
schoolbag die Schultasche
scissors die Schere
Scotland Schottland
sea das Meer, die See
seashell die Muschel

season die Jahreszeit
to see sehen
to sell verkaufen
September der September
seven sieben
to shake schütteln
sheep das Schaf
shelves das Regal
sheriff der Sheriff
to shine scheinen
ship das Schiff
shoe der Schuh
shop das Geschäft, der Laden
shopping der Einkauf, das Einkaufen
short kurz
shorts die kurze Hose
shoulder die Schulter
to show zeigen
sick krank
to sing singen
sister die Schwester
six sechs
skirt der Rock
sleigh der (Pferde-)Schlitten
slow langsam
small klein
to smell riechen
snake die Schlange
to snorkel schnorcheln, tauchen
snow der Schnee
snowboarding das Snowboarden
snowman der Schneemann
snowy verschneit
sock die Socke
sofa das Sofa
song das Lied
I'm sorry! Entschuldigung!
soup die Suppe
spaceship das Raumschiff
Spain Spanien
to speak sprechen
spider die Spinne
spinach der Spinat
spoon der Löffel
sports Sport
spring der Frühling
stairs die Treppe
to stamp stampfen
star der Stern
stereo die Musikanlage
stocking der Strumpf
story die Geschichte
strong stark
sugar der Zucker
summer der Sommer
sun die Sonne
Sunday der Sonntag
sunglasses die Sonnenbrille
sunny sonnig
sweatshirt das Sweatshirt
sweet süß
sweets die Süßigkeiten
to swim schwimmen

table der Tisch
tadpole die Kaulquappe
to take nehmen
to take off ausziehen
tall groß
taxi das Taxi
tea der Tee
teacher der Lehrer, die Lehrerin
teddy bear der Teddybär
teeth die Zähne
ten zehn
Thank you! Danke!
Thanksgiving Day das Erntedankfest
thirsty durstig
three drei

Words

Thursday der Donnerstag
to tidy aufräumen, saubermachen
tired müde
toast der Toast
toe der Zeh
toilet die Toilette, das Klo
tomato (tomatoes)
die Tomate (die Tomaten)
tooth der Zahn
tortoise die Schildkröte
to touch anfassen
towel das Handtuch
toy das Spielzeug
train der Zug
tree der Baum
trousers die Hose
T-shirt das T-Shirt
Tuesday der Dienstag
turkey der Truthahn
twelve zwölf
two zwei

uncle der Onkel
under unter
underground die U-Bahn
unhappy unglücklich
Union Jack britische Fahne
United States of America
die Vereinigten Staaten von Amerika,
die USA
up hinauf

Valentine's Day der Valentinstag
vehicle das Fahrzeug, das Verkehrsmittel

to walk gehen, wandern
to walk the dog
den Hund spazieren führen
to write schreiben
warm warm
water das Wasser
to wash waschen
wax figure die Wachsfigur
to wear tragen
weather das Wetter
weather forecast
die Wettervorhersage
Wednesday der Mittwoch
white weiß
wild wild
wind der Wind
window das Fenster
windy windig
winter der Winter
witch die Hexe
woolly hat die Mütze
word das Wort
workbook das Arbeitsheft

yellow gelb